PARLIAMENT AND
ITS BUILDINGS

Richard Tames

SHIRE PUBLICATIONS

Published in Great Britain in 2012 by Shire Publications
Ltd, Midland House, West Way, Botley, Oxford OX2 0PH,
United Kingdom.

43-01 21st Street, Suite 220B, Long Island City, NY 11101,
USA.

E-mail: shire@shirebooks.co.uk   www.shirebooks.co.uk

A CIP catalogue record for this book is available from the
British Library.

Shire Library no. 696.   ISBN-13: 978 0 74781 166 4

Richard Tames has asserted his right under the Copyright,
Designs and Patents Act, 1988, to be identified as the
author of this book.

Designed by Tony Truscott Designs, Sussex, UK
and typeset in Perpetua and Gill Sans.

Printed in China through Worldprint Ltd.

12 13 14 15 16   10 9 8 7 6 5 4 3 2 1

COVER IMAGE
The House of Lords took possession of its chamber,
Pugin's masterpiece, in 1847.

TITLE PAGE IMAGE
The House of Commons was slightly modified when it was
rebuilt by Sir Giles Gilbert Scott after it was bombed in
1940. It closely resembles the Victorian chamber shown
on page 41.

CONTENTS PAGE IMAGE
A detail from the arch of the Sovereign's Entrance, situated
at the bottom of the Victoria Tower. Heraldic roses of the
Tudor monarchs flank three angels, which support
the royal arms.

ACKNOWLEDGEMENTS
Illustrations are acknowledged as follows:
Alamy, pages 10, 15, 16, 18, 21 (both), 26, 32, and 42–3;
Russell Butcher, contents page and pages 4, 6 (top),
9 (top), 17, 25, 31, 33 (bottom), 34 (top), 35 (both), 40,
56, 58 (bottom) and 62 (top); Ben Cooper, page 36–7
(bottom); Jim Ebdon, pages 22, 23 (bottom) and 45;
Getty Images, page 44; Steve James, page 14; Library of
Congress, pages 19 and 24 (top); Fr Lawrence Lew, O. P.,
page 6 (bottom); Terry Moore, front cover and page 57;
National Portrait Gallery, page 33 (top two);
Peter Matthews, pages 20 (bottom) and 23 (top);
Parliamentary copyright, title page and pages 8 (bottom),
9 (bottom left and bottom right), 29 (both), 30, 34
(bottom), 37 (top), 38, 39, 41 (bottom), 46, 48, 52–3, 55,
and 58 (top); Bill Scott, page 60–1 (top); James Stringer,
page 12; Richard Tames, pages 7 (both), 8 (top), 20 (top),
24 (bottom), 28, 41 (top), 51, 59 (both), 62 (bottom).

Shire Publications is supporting the Woodland Trust, the UK's leading woodland conservation charity, by funding the dedication of trees.

CONTENTS

THE 'MOTHER OF PARLIAMENTS'

PARLIAMENT stands at the heart of Britain's history, the source and crucible of its gift to the world – governance through liberty under the law. Legally speaking, Parliament consists of the monarch, the House of Lords, and the House of Commons, each of which must give its consent to the making of a law – 'Be it enacted by the Queen's most excellent Majesty, by and with the advice and consent of the Lords Spiritual and Temporal, and Commons...'. Constitutional practice requires Her Majesty's Government to have the support of a majority of the 650 elected members of the House of Commons – Members of Parliament, known as MPs – for the duration of a parliament, a term of not more than five years. MPs also provide the pool from which almost all government ministers are drawn. Parliament's other major function is to examine, discuss, criticise, amend and sometimes reject government proposals, whether for implementing a policy or creating new legislation. The House of Commons works in collaboration with the House of Lords, also known as the House of Peers – or 'the Other Place' – which once constituted the senior partner in their relationship but is now the ancillary element.

The word 'parliament' derives from the Old French *parlement*, meaning 'speaking'. In English by 1542 'parliament' had also acquired the deeper meaning of 'debate' or 'discussion'. As consultative assemblies summoned by rulers, parliaments emerged in many kingdoms of medieval Europe, but most died out with the trend to absolute monarchy. In France the parliamentary element of government, the States-General, was not convened between 1614 and 1789, when its hasty recall marked the first fatal step towards revolution. In Britain, by contrast, during that same period Parliament confirmed its supremacy over the monarchy as the dominant element in the constitutional arrangements that shaped how the country should be governed.

Originally meeting when and wherever it was summoned, Parliament evolved into a more regular component of royal governance and by the fourteenth century assembled most frequently in the precincts of the monarch's

Opposite:
The clock tower of the Houses of Parliament, often incorrectly referred to as 'Big Ben', stands 316 feet high. The roof needed four thousand books of gold leaf to decorate it.

St Margaret's, Westminster, built about 1482–1523, has been the parish church of the House of Commons since 1614, its clergy usually providing the Speaker's chaplain. Famous people married at St Margaret's include John Milton and Sir Winston Churchill. John Pym, leader of the parliamentary opposition to Charles I, is buried here.

Westminster Hall is 240 feet long and 68 feet wide. The unsupported hammerbeam roof (1394–1401), the largest in the country, is 92 feet high and weighs 660 tons. Steel strengthening was skilfully inserted in the 1920s. The floor area is 1,850 square yards.

The Gothic architecture of Canada's parliament building in Ottawa, built between 1860 and 1876, both echoed the style of its Westminster counterpart and deliberately contrasted with the classical style chosen for the Congress of the republican United States in Washington DC.

palace at Westminster, a medieval partnership echoed in the formal designation of the present Houses of Parliament as the 'New Palace of Westminster'. Following a disastrous fire in 1834, the Houses of Parliament were rebuilt in a medieval Gothic style, deliberately chosen to represent the long continuity of their past existence. The outcome was an architectural triumph, which became a symbol of the nation itself. Together with the adjacent Westminster Abbey and church of St Margaret, the Houses of Parliament were designated a UNESCO World Heritage site in 1987, for illustrating 'in colossal form the grandeur of constitutional monarchy', and representing 'an outstanding, coherent and complete example of neo-Gothic syle'. The roof of ancient Westminster Hall was singled out as 'one of the greatest achievements of medieval construction in wood', and the entire complex praised for the cumulative effect of nine

A paddle-steamer carries tourists past the majestic river frontage of the Houses of Parliament. The Tsar of Russia called the building 'a dream in stone' and Adolf Hitler referred to it in *Mein Kampf* as 'Barry's masterpiece'.

The chimes of Big Ben, lasting 95 seconds, imitate those of the church of the University of Cambridge, Great St Mary's, set to the following lines: 'All through this hour, / Lord, be my guide, / And by thy power, / No foot shall slide.'

centuries of taste and craftsmanship – 'Art is everywhere present and harmonious, making a veritable museum of the history of the United Kingdom.'

The Westminster parliament has been the model for many other parliamentary systems, especially those of Commonwealth countries such as Canada and Australia. When Brazil – never a British colony – adopted parliamentary institutions in the nineteenth century, members wore tight-fitting frock coats and top hats despite the sweltering climate, because that was how it was done at Westminster.

Westminster's global influence is symbolised by Commonwealth contributions to the reconstruction of Parliament after the destruction of the House of Commons during the Blitz: the Speaker's chair is made of Australian wood, the Table of the House is Canadian oak, the bronze Bar of the House was a gift from Jamaica, and the entrance doors to the chamber were given by India and Pakistan.

'Big Ben' is actually the bell (weighing 13.8 tonnes) that strikes the hours and quarters, *not* the clock or the tower. It may be named after Sir Benjamin Hall, Commissioner of Works, who supervised the building of the present Houses of Parliament, or possibly the boxer Benjamin Caunt.

The dials of the great Westminster clock are 23 feet across. The centres are 180 feet above the ground. The hollow copper minute hands, weighing 2cwt, are 14 feet long and travel 100 miles a year. The 9-foot hour hands, weighing 6cwt, are solid gun-metal.

Left: The interior of one of the dials of the great clock – the hands of all four are driven from a single movement. The bulbs which illuminate the dial at night can be seen on the wall to the right. Tours of the clock are free on application to UK permanent residents aged eleven or over.

Below: The staircase in the Clock Tower has 384 steps.

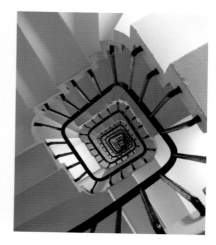

THE EVOLUTION OF PARLIAMENT

W ISE KINGS rule with the support of the powerful. Anglo-Saxon monarchs consulted a *witanegemot* (*witan* = wise men; *gemot* = assembly) of great lords. Although it had no fixed membership or meeting-place, this played a key role in endorsing succession to the throne and was a distant ancestor of the House of Lords, the privy council and the courts of law. The Anglo-Norman kings who ruled after 1066 also consulted a King's Council (*Curia Regis*) of barons, often at Westminster, although irregularly.

Persistent abuses of royal power by King John (1199–1216) provoked a baronial rebellion that forced the king to accept the barons' demands, summarised in a Great Charter (*Magna Carta*), which he sealed at Runnymede in 1215. The document's most important principles were that the king was as much bound by the law as his subjects, and that his powers to make laws and raise taxes involved the consent of 'the community of the realm'. John had no intention of keeping his word but his death soon after led to the reissuing of the charter by subsequent monarchs at their succession as a pledge of good governance. Later generations exalted the status of Magna Carta from an aborted peace treaty to the foundation document of Anglo-American liberties – so revered that the four surviving copies (at Lincoln and Salisbury cathedrals, and two in the British Library) have special UNESCO World Heritage status.

Parliament – the word was first used in 1236 – emerged in the long and turbulent reign of Henry III (1216–72) as an assembly of the three estates of the realm: those who fought, those who prayed, and those who worked – barons, clergy, and commons, the last representing not commoners but *communes* (communities). In 1254 sheriffs, the king's representative in each county, were ordered each to send two knights of the shire to advise the king on finance. In 1265 the rebel Simon de Montfort summoned a parliament – in the name of the king, his brother-in-law Henry III – to meet at Westminster, composed of peers (nobles), bishops, abbots, knights of the shire, and burgesses from chartered boroughs.

Opposite: Speaker Lenthall declines to comply with Charles I's demand to identify leaders of the parliamentary opposition to his rule. The results of the Civil Wars, in which Parliament and the king fought for supremacy, had a marked influence on the development of parliament.

The 'Model Parliament' (1295) of Edward I (1272–1307) crystallised its basic components. The House of Clergy represented only lesser churchmen. Bishops and abbots sat with – and outnumbered – the seven earls and forty-one barons in the House of Lords, whose members were summoned by name, rather than as representatives chosen by others. Members of the House of Commons included two knights from each shire, two burgesses from each borough, and two citizens from each cathedral city, all elected rather than appointed. Unlike his father, Henry III, Edward I worked with Parliament to exercise royal authority, summoning forty-six parliaments in a reign of thirty-five years.

A procedural handbook, the *Modus Tenendi Parliamentum* ('Method of Holding a Parliament'), compiled in the troubled reign of Edward II (1307–27), emphasised that peers attended Parliament 'for themselves in their own person and no other', whereas knights and burgesses were to 'represent the whole community of England'.

Between the accession of Edward III (1327–77) and 1338, only thirteen of twenty-nine parliaments met at Westminster; from 1339 until the end of his reign, all thirty-one did. From 1332 the Lords and Commons met separately for their deliberations. In 1362 a statute declared that all taxation of non-clergy had to be approved by Parliament. In 1407 Henry IV acknowledged that tax proposals had to be raised first in the Commons. In 1414 Henry V acknowledged that the king could accept or reject a bill drafted

From 1352 the House of Commons sat in the chapter house of Westminster Abbey.

by the Commons but not alter it. Thus, by the acceptance and accumulation of precedent, rather than by any predetermined plan, the structure and functions of Parliament and its component parts became more formalised as it asserted its power in relation to the monarchy.

While the members of the Lords expected to be consulted by the king, the members of the other houses probably thought attendance was more a chore than a privilege. Fortunately it did not happen often or for long. England's medieval parliament was an occasion, rather than a permanent institution. Summoned by the monarch for his own ends – to raise taxes for a foreign war, or to punish threats or challenges to royal authority, it convened for brief periods of intense and varied activity: judging cases, receiving petitions, serving more as a forum for proclaiming new laws than as an instrument for making them. In return for supporting and justifying the royal will with the endorsement of communal approval, Parliament – usually the Commons – increasingly sought a return through the remedy of general grievances or the granting of specific rights or favours. From 1363, however, 1the Commons had the services of a clerk in the conduct of its business. The office of Speaker, dating from 1376, originally meant acting as spokesman to the king but evolved into controlling the fair conduct of debates.

The proceedings of Parliament were opened in English for the first time in 1362, while written documentation in the form of 'petitions of the Commons' began to be in English from 1423 onwards, and by the 1480s parliamentary statutes in their final form were cast in English. The Rolls of Parliament, an official royal summary of proceedings, kept from the reign of Edward I, were originally recorded entirely in Latin, switching to Anglo-Norman and Middle English before being superseded by records kept by the Lords and Commons themselves.

By 1400 Parliament had acquired two key functions: to grant taxes, and to pass statutes. The king with his advisors serving as a great or privy council could issue ordinances, but these were essentially laws that were either temporary or concerned with detail, not permanent or general. The monarch could neither suspend nor revoke statutes, although he could exempt particular individuals from particular laws. When Richard II (1377–99) abused such power, he was deposed by Henry IV (1399-1413). Having only a weak claim to the throne, Henry ensured that the transition was endorsed by Parliament, hiding a brutal overthrow behind a façade of smooth continuity. In 1414 Henry V accepted that the Lords and Commons had equal powers over lawmaking, a recognition of the emerging significance of the supposedly subordinate house.

Parliament was held at the king's initiative, usually when he needed extra money for a war or an ambitious building programme. Rich and thrifty kings could largely do without parliaments. Henry VII summoned only seven, sitting for a total of just twenty-five weeks in his whole reign (1485–1509). Kings could also manipulate parliaments by dissolving or proroguing (suspending) troublesome ones, and by creating new peers or parliamentary boroughs.

England's parliament was unusual in having its lesser clergy opt out to meet in separate bodies, the Convocations of Canterbury and York, which concerned themselves with church matters and the separate taxation of the clergy. Bishops and, until the Reformation, abbots continued to sit with the Lords. Peculiarly, knights sat alongside burgesses, not with the nobles.

Paradoxically it was the authoritarian Henry VIII (1509–47) who effectively – if not intentionally – strengthened Parliament by using it to endorse his revolutionary break with Rome, declaring that 'we be informed by our judges that we at no time stand so highly in our estate royal as in the time of Parliament, wherein we as head and you as members are conjoined and knit together as one body politic'. Under Henry VIII Parliament sat repeatedly (1529–36) to pass statutes asserting the supremacy of the king, rather than the Pope, over the Church; to endorse his plundering of its properties by dissolving the monasteries and abbeys; and to incorporate Wales into the kingdom, with its own members going to Parliament at Westminster. The first known committee (1529) dates from this period, as does the first vote by division (1532), when MPs physically separated into different areas for their votes for or against a proposition to be counted – as they still do when necessary.

Sir Thomas More (1478–1535) served as Speaker of the House of Commons and Henry VIII's chief minister, but resigned rather than accept the king's supremacy over the Church. Executed for treason, More was canonised in 1935 and made patron saint of politicians in 2000. His statue stands outside Chelsea Old Church.

Henry VIII's son and successor, Edward VI (1547–53), gave the Commons a new home in the deconsecrated chapel of St Stephen, where it remained until the fire of 1834. The custom of having members sit opposite each other in stalls, like a monastic choir, may have encouraged the evolution of a more adversarial style of debate than if they had been ranged in ranks behind each other or in a horseshoe shape. As Sir Winston Churchill observed, 'We shape our buildings and afterwards our buildings shape us.' Another parliamentary milestone was passed in 1547 as the Commons inaugurated the practice of keeping journals as a record of its proceedings, creating a collective memory of its procedures and privileges.

Henry VIII's daughter, Elizabeth I (1558–1603), summoned only ten parliaments in a reign of forty-five years, sitting for a total of 140 weeks. Sittings, six days a week, were from 8 o'clock until 11 o'clock in the morning, with afternoons free for committee meetings. When Parliament did meet, the queen could scold it in person as well as cajole or flatter, but more usually she relied on members of her privy council to influence its debates to reach the outcome she wanted. Failing all else, she had individual offenders suspended or imprisoned. Nevertheless Sir Thomas Smith could assert in his *De Republica Anglorum* ('Concerning the English State') that Parliament could abrogate old laws, make new ones, grant pardons, alter property rights and even change religion, because 'the consent of Parliament is taken to be every man's consent'. His recipe for good rule, however, was 'peace, liberty, quietness, little taking of money, few Parliaments'.

Roman Catholics were disappointed when the son of the devoutly Catholic Mary, Queen of Scots, the Protestant James I (1603–25), failed to ease laws restricting their worship. A Catholic conspiracy to blow up the king at the State Opening of Parliament on 5 November 1605 was infiltrated and foiled. Conspirators Robert Catesby and Thomas Percy fled and were killed resisting arrest. Robert Winter and Guy Fawkes, the ex-mercenary tasked with setting the explosion, were tortured, tried in Westminster Hall for treason, and hanged, drawn and quartered. 5 November has since then been celebrated annually as 'Guy Fawkes Night' with fireworks and the burning of a 'guy' on a bonfire. For 250 years afterwards parliamentarians attended a service of thanksgiving at St Margaret's, Westminster. The gunpowder was later shown to have decayed and would not have exploded.

James I found the larger and more formal English parliament much harder to manage than its Scottish equivalent, but it was during his reign that the right of the Commons to settle disputed elections and its own procedures was finally confirmed. Similar difficulties led

A former soldier in the army of Catholic Spain, Guy ('Guido') Fawkes (1570–1605) was the explosives expert for the 'Gunpowder Plot' to blow up Parliament.

Ciuitatis Weſtmonaſteriensis pars.

Parlament Houſe · the Hall · the Abby ·

The Czech artist Wenceslas Hollar's depiction of Westminster in 1643 shows a jumble of riverside buildings overshadowed by the former St Stephen's Chapel (labelled Parliament House) and Westminster Hall.

Charles I (1625–49) to rule without Parliament from 1629 onwards. For the following sixty years there was a see-saw struggle for supremacy between Crown and Parliament.

Charles I's personal rule ended in 1640 when his ill-judged interference in Scotland's religious life provoked a Scottish invasion of England, forcing him to call a parliament to grant money to raise an army. Parliament's accumulated grievances and the king's intransigence created a stalemate leading to outright civil war. In January 1642 Charles I, with armed soldiers, tried to seize five of his leading critics in the House of Commons. Speaker Lenthall quietly defied the king's order to identify them (see page 10), memorably saying 'I have neither eyes to see nor tongue to speak in this place but as this House hath pleased to direct me, whose servant I am here...'. In fact the five members had already fled. No reigning monarch has entered the House of Commons since.

The Civil Wars (1642–9), embroiling England, Scotland, Ireland and Wales, ended with the defeat of the king and his trial by Parliament for treason in making war on his own people. Following the execution of the king, the monarchy itself was abolished, along with the House of Lords. A depleted House of Commons continued to sit as a self-perpetuating 'Rump Parliament'.

After failed experiments with direct parliamentary and military rule, the victorious parliamentary commander and former MP Oliver Cromwell ruled as 'Lord Protector' (1653–8), king in all but name, until his death; but he failed to devise a satisfactory form of government or provide for an effective succession. After Cromwell's death the constitutional vacuum was filled by inviting the late king's son to return from exile as Charles II (1660–85) and reinstating the House of Lords. The outcome of the Civil Wars was thus an uncertain compromise, with the monarchy chastened, but the limits of royal power not yet bounded by a definitive constitutional settlement. Although Charles professed to finding Parliament 'better than a play', he resisted its repeated efforts to bar his brother James, a convert to Roman Catholicism, from succeeding to the throne. Accepting a secret subsidy from Louis XIV of France, in 1681 he summoned Parliament to Oxford – far from the threat of the London mob – just to dismiss it, and to reign without one until his death.

James II (1685–88) did, indeed, succeed his brother but when he appointed Catholics to senior positions in the army, Church and universities,

The statue of Oliver Cromwell was unveiled in 1899 to mark the three-hundredth anniversary of his birth. Even then, he was still such a controversial figure that it had to be erected outside Parliament, to the west of Westminster Hall, which can be seen here in the backgound.

Britain's most famous front door. Until the 1980s tourists could take photographs right in front of No. 10 Downing Street, but since then the street has been sealed off by security gates and guarded by armed police.

and suspended the laws limiting Catholic rights, his Protestant daughter Mary was invited to take the throne alongside her Dutch husband, William, subject to accepting the supremacy of Parliament. James fled into exile. This bloodless 'Glorious Revolution' of 1688–9 inaugurated a new and unique phenomenon – 'limited monarchy' – as the Crown lost its power to suspend statutes and to keep a standing army in peacetime without consent of Parliament. The 1689 Bill of Rights also asserted Parliament's rights to free elections and free debate. In 1694, to ensure regular meetings of Parliament, the Triennial Act required that it should meet at least once every three years and last no more than three years. The following rapid turnover of parliaments caused ruinous expense to candidates at elections until the interval was increased to seven years in 1716.

Parliament confirmed its supremacy in 1701 by passing the Act of Settlement, which determined who should succeed to the throne after the death of the childless William and Mary. It also forbade the sovereign to leave England without Parliament's permission. In 1707 an Act of Union was passed, abolishing Scotland's separate parliament in return for proportionately over-representing Scotland's population at Westminster, and acknowledging the continued separateness of Scotland's church and legal system.

After the death of Queen Anne (1702–14) the throne passed to a Protestant German prince, George of Hanover, who as George I (1714–27) never mastered English and eventually left the day-to-day conduct of politics to his ministers, meeting as a 'Cabinet' chaired by the First Lord of the Treasury, informally known as the prime minister. The first holder of the office, Sir Robert Walpole (1676–1745), held power for two decades (1721–42) by managing the House of Commons through skilful use of appointments, favours and bribes. In 1735 George II (1727–60) presented Walpole with No. 10 Downing Street, which has been the official residence of the prime minister ever since.

Elections became routinely corrupt as open voting and the small numbers qualified to vote made it easy to buy or coerce electors in hundreds of what became known as 'rotten boroughs', because the right to represent them in Parliament was in the gift of a local grandee. The controllers of rotten boroughs could thus act as faction leaders in Parliament. Other factions represented powerful economic interests, such as the East India Company or the owners of Caribbean slave plantations. Some rural areas, such as Cornwall, had dozens of MPs, while emerging industrial cities such as Manchester and Birmingham had none. In 1785 the Bill introduced by Prime Minister William Pitt (1759–1806) to disfranchise thirty-six rotten boroughs was thrown out by the House of Commons. With the outbreak of war with revolutionary France in 1792,

DRAWN BY GRAVELOT

HOUSE of COMMONS,

ENGRAVED BY W. J. WHITE.

as it appeared in 1741.

The House of Commons in 1741, as depicted by the French artist H. F. Gravelot. Britain's freedom of debate was admired by foreign visitors such as Voltaire.

In 1776 former naval officer and militia major John Cartwright published *Take Your Choice!*, arguing the case for manhood suffrage, paid MPs, secret voting, equal constituencies and annual elections. He also raised a fund for widows and orphans of Americans killed at Lexington and Concord and campaigned against slavery.

JOHN CARTWRIGHT,
BORN 28 SEP 1740 DIED 23 SEP 1824.
The Firm, Consistent & Persevering Advocate of
UNIVERSAL SUFFRAGE,
Equal Representation. Vote by Ballot.
AND
ANNUAL PARLIAMENTS.
He was the first English Writer who openly maintained
the Independence of the United States of America:
AND
Although his distinguished Merits as a Naval Officer
in 1776 presented the most flattering Prospects of
Professional Advancement,
yet he nobly refused to draw his Sword against
the Rising Liberties
of an oppressed and struggling People.
In Grateful Commemoration
of his inflexible integrity, exalted Patriotism,
profound constitutional Knowledge,
and in sincere admiration
of the unblemished Virtues of his Private Life
THIS STATUE
Was erected by Public Subscription,
near the Spot
where he closed his useful and meritorious
CAREER.

reform was set aside for a generation. A failed national uprising in Ireland (1798) led to the abolition of the Irish parliament (1800) and the addition of one hundred Irish MPs to the House of Commons.

As the memory of the French Revolution faded, demands grew for a fairer and more efficient parliamentary system to meet the needs of a nation changing rapidly under the impact of urbanisation and industrialisation. In 1818 a House of Commons library was established as a resource for members. In 1829 Roman Catholics were at last granted full civil liberties, including the right to be elected as MPs. Jews gained the same right in 1858.

Nationwide agitation and riots persuaded Prime Minister Lord Grey (1764–1845) to introduce the Great Reform Act of 1832 to head off the threat of revolution. This abolished fifty-six English rotten boroughs and deprived thirty more with fewer than four thousand residents of one of their members. New constituencies were allocated to reflect more accurately the proportion of population in the counties (65), large towns (44), smaller towns (21), Scotland (8), and Ireland (5). The vote was extended to property-holders making up about a fifth of the male population. Registers of voters were henceforth to be compiled.

John Wilkes (1727–97) attacked the power of the Crown, calling for parliamentary reform. A womanising rake, duellist and pornographer, Wilkes nevertheless became Lord Mayor of London and was re-elected an MP after being twice expelled from Parliament. His statue stands in Fetter Lane, off Fleet Street.

The Reform Act may have headed off revolution, but it created discontent among the still excluded working classes. Chartism was the outcome, a mass movement whose broad appeal was matched by confusion in its leadership and strategy. The 1838 'People's Charter', for which it was named, demanded votes for all men; annual parliamentary elections; voting by secret ballot; the abolition of property

This 1832 cartoon shows Lord Grey and his supporters wielding axes of reform against rotten boroughs, while the reactionary Duke of Wellington (in the red coat) vainly leads the resistance of vested interests seeking to prop up a discredited system of representation.

qualifications for MPs; payment of MPs; and equal electoral districts. Chartist tactics included mass petitions, an abortive 'national convention' (i.e. a People's Parliament), and an equally abortive 'national holiday' (a general strike). A mass meeting called to Kennington Common in 1848 prompted elaborate preparations for defending London from a feared uprising, with eighty thousand men enrolled as special constables, but the demonstrators dispersed peaceably and Chartism fizzled out, although the movement did

The great Chartist demonstration on Kennington Common in 1848. Extensive precautions were made to defend Parliament from a feared assault, but the demonstrators dispersed peaceably and the Chartist movement faded away.

Sir Robert Peel (1788–1850), Britain's first middle-class prime minister, was the founder of the modern Conservative party and of London's Metropolitan Police, and abolished many restrictions on trade and industry. His statue on Parliament Square stands near Westminster Abbey.

produce many future leaders of trade unions, the temperance crusade and working-class projects for self-improvement.

The period between the First and Second Reform Acts has been regarded by some historians as a golden age for Parliament. Because parties were fluid and their control over individual MPs was correspondingly weak, the House of Commons enjoyed more power over its proceedings, priorities and timetable than ever before or since. Government proposals for legislation were often greatly amended or even thrown out. Individual ministers could be hounded out of office for incompetence or offending the House. Instead of reaching a foregone conclusion, debates were unpredictable and could even lead to the fall of a government that had lost the confidence of the Commons. Other historians, however, have seen this phase as a temporary aberration, with strong party control by the government side as the historical norm. In 1860 only 7 per cent of votes were 'party' votes, when 90 per cent or more of the members of a party all voted the same way; by 1881 76 per cent of votes were party votes.

Renewed working-class agitation and fears of disorder eventually led to the passage of the Second Reform Act (1867), which redistributed fifty-three seats and extended the vote to the skilled working class, increasing the electorate to one male in three. The introduction of voting by secret ballot in 1872 ended the power of employers and landlords to direct the votes of employees and tenants. A Third Reform Act (1884) extended the franchise in rural areas but, even so, some 40 per cent of males remained unregistered to vote. Nevertheless, the enlargement of the electorate to more than five million obliged political parties to create mass-membership organisations outside Parliament to mobilise their votes. The growth of the trade-union movement provided a launch pad from which an infant Labour Party emerged after 1900.

In 1909 the House of Lords, dominated by Conservative aristocrats, rejected the provocative 'People's Budget' presented by the Liberal

Chancellor of the Exchequer, David Lloyd George, which proposed new taxes on motor cars and land sales, directly hitting the rich. Two general elections and a threat by George V (1910–36) to create hundreds of new peers to force through the budget were needed before the Lords gave way. The supremacy of the Commons in matters of finance was confirmed by the Parliament Act of 1911, which limited the Lords' power to delay money bills to one month, and other bills to two years (reduced to one in 1949). The same Act reduced the length of Parliaments from seven years to five. Also in 1911, an annual salary for MPs of £400 a year was introduced, opening up the possibility of a parliamentary career for those who were not independently wealthy or sponsored by a trade union.

The constitutional expert James Bryce thought the idea of giving women the vote was 'an experiment so large and bold that it ought to be tried by some other country first'. That was in 1892 – and New Zealand did just that in 1893. Parliament first debated giving British women the vote in 1867, but it took half a century to achieve this. 'Suffragists' advocated a gradualist approach, encouraged by small successes such as winning female property-holders the vote in local elections and the right to sit on school boards. From 1906 onwards, militant 'suffragettes' adopted radical tactics ranging from heckling to arson, many suffering imprisonment for acts of disruption and destruction. On the night of the census, 2 April 1911, the suffragette Emily Davison successfully hid herself in a broom cupboard in the Undercroft Chapel so that she could give her address as the House of Commons – where she thought women ought to be by right. She was killed in 1913 at the Derby when she ran on to the course in front of the king's horse, flourishing a suffragette flag. The issue of women's suffrage remained unresolved when war broke out in 1914, but the contribution made by women to the war effort transformed public attitudes.

Oddly, the Representation of the People Act (1918) gave women the right to stand for Parliament at twenty-one, but the vote only at

Originally a Conservative, but four times prime minister as a Liberal, William Gladstone (1809–98) modernised the army, civil service, law courts and local government. A learned scholar and formidable speaker, he was renowned for his strong religious and political principles. His statue stands in the middle of Bow Road.

Gladstone's arch-rival, Benjamin Disraeli, Earl of Beaconsfield (1804–81), was Britain's first Jewish prime minister. Pragmatic and witty, he made the Conservatives a party of progress. A best-selling novelist, he excelled in debate and parliamentary manoeuvring.

Suffragettes attract curious male stares. As their tactics became more militant, suffragettes encountered fierce hostility and even violence at the hands of mobs – and sometimes the police.

The Refreshment Room of the Victorian House of Lords – an elegant setting for the exchange of political rumours and gossip. Notice the custom of wearing hats inside Parliament.

thirty, although this was lowered to twenty-one in 1928. The Act also enfranchised all men over twenty-one, subject to six months fixed residency in a constituency, and also abolished all property qualifications. Together these provisions increased the electorate from 8 million to 21 million. The first woman MP to take her seat was Nancy, Viscountess Astor (1879–1964), in 1919. The first woman cabinet minister (1929–31) was Margaret Bondfield (1873–1953).

In 1974 Margaret Thatcher declared that 'It will be years before a woman either leads the Party or becomes prime minister. I certainly do not expect to see it happening in my lifetime.' But she became leader of the Conservative party the following year, and Britain's first woman prime minister in 1979. In 1992 Betty Boothroyd (born 1929) became the first woman Speaker of the House of Commons.

LATE-TWENTIETH-CENTURY DEVELOPMENTS

1948 Representation of the People Act: separate seats for universities abolished.

1958 Life Peerages Act: created non-hereditary peerages and admitted women to the House of Lords.

1961 Prime Minister's Question Time introduced (then held twice weekly).

1963 Peerage Act: enables peers to disclaim their titles so they can stand for election to the Commons.

1967 Parliamentary Commissioner (Ombudsman) established to investigate allegations of unjust or incompetent administration by government departments.

1969 Voting age lowered from twenty-one to eighteen.

1985 UK citizens resident overseas granted the right to vote for fifteen years.

1999 The number of hereditary peers in the House of Lords limited to ninety-two.

1999 Scottish Parliament and Welsh National Assembly established.

The militant suffragette campaign was co-ordinated by the Women's Social and Political Union (WSPU), led by Mrs Emmeline Pankhurst (1858–1928), who was imprisoned a dozen times, went on hunger strike and suffered forced feeding. After women got the vote Mrs Pankhurst failed to become an MP. Her statue stands beside the Victoria Tower.

THE PALACE OF WESTMINSTER

PARLIAMENT STANDS on a triangular site once called Thorney Island, a desolate place thick with brambles and bounded by the River Thames and two streams that still flow underground from the direction of St James's Park station. Known to neolithic hunters, Bronze Age farmers and Roman invaders, it was probably the location of a small church by the seventh century and was the site of a Benedictine abbey by the tenth.

A royal palace was established at Westminster by the Danish king Knut (Canute) (1016–35), from which he ruled an Anglo-Scandinavian maritime empire. This palace was greatly enlarged when Anglo-Saxon rule was re-established under the saintly Edward the Confessor (1042–66), so that he could supervise the rebuilding of the abbey as a grand project in the Norman (Romanesque) style, modelled on the abbey at Jumièges in Normandy. Edward died within weeks of the abbey's completion and was buried there. The abbey was substantially rebuilt by Henry III between 1245 and 1269, although alterations and additions continued for a further five centuries.

William the Conqueror (1066–87) asserted his right to the succession by being crowned in the abbey, enlarging the palace and entertaining there lavishly. His son William II ('Rufus', 1087–1100), commandeered forced labour to build Westminster Hall as the architectural marvel of the age. Constructed in 1097–9, it was the largest hall in England, probably in Europe, and served as the ceremonial centre of the kingdom for a thousand years. The palace decayed during the anarchic reign of Stephen (1135–54), but was restored by the dynamic Henry II (1154–89).

King John (1199–1216) made Westminster the permanent site of the Exchequer, the government's finance and taxation department, and of the courts of King's Bench and Common Pleas, joined by Chancery, the Crown's administrative office, by 1310. John's son, Henry III (1216–72), an extravagant aesthete, made Westminster the most dazzling royal palace in Europe, complete with a royal bath in the form of a jewel-encrusted peacock – although he was powerless to protect the palace from floods (1236 and 1242), fire (1263) or London mobs on the rampage (1257 and 1267).

Opposite:
The Prince's Chamber. In contrast to the surrounding Tudor and Gothic motifs, the pedestal of Queen Victoria's statue depicts state-of-the-art technology – a steam engine and telegraph wires.

WESTMINSTER HALL

Westminster Hall was the scene of many historic events, including:

1295 Edward I's Model Parliament.
1305 Trial of Sir William Wallace ('Braveheart').
1327 Abdication of Edward II.
1399 Deposition of Richard II.
1461 Accession of Edward IV.
1535 Trial of Sir Thomas More.
1605 Trial of Guy Fawkes.
1649 Trial of Charles I.
1653 Inauguration of Oliver Cromwell as Lord Protector.

Traditionally after coronations a celebration banquet was held in Westminster Hall. At the last, held for George IV in 1821, the offerings included 2,140 bottles of wine, 100 gallons of iced punch, 100 barrels of beer and 8 tons of poultry and meats.

The Lords and Commons have assembled in Westminster Hall to hear addresses by General de Gaulle, Nelson Mandela and Presidents Reagan and Obama. Here also thousands have queued patiently to honour the lying-in-state of William Gladstone, Edward VII, George VI, Winston Churchill and Queen Elizabeth the Queen Mother.

A pre-war aerial view of Westminster with the Treasury building in the left foreground. Most of the pavilions of St Thomas's Hospital on the far side of the Thames were destroyed in the Blitz. More than a thousand years of development have changed Thorney Island beyond recognition.

This imaginative reconstruction of Westminster Hall as originally built in the reign of William II shows how massive columns were then needed to support the roof.

Now used mainly for ceremonial occasions, Westminster Hall also housed the main law courts until 1882, and was for centuries crammed with sellers of books, stationery, wigs and snacks, giving it the look of a fashionable shopping mall.

The royal residence lay south and east of Westminster Hall, incorporating a Painted Chamber, serving as the royal bedroom and audience room, whose gorgeous murals took sixty years to complete. For royal devotions, St Stephen's Chapel was built over seventy years (1292–1363) in imitation

of the Sainte Chapelle in Paris. 90 feet long and 100 feet high, it was completed by Edward III (1327–77) at a cost of £9,000, equivalent to the budget for a castle. Beneath it, for lesser members of the royal entourage, was the Chapel of St Mary Undercroft, which has subsequently served as a stable, coal cellar, wine store, and a dining-room for the Speaker of the House of Commons, and which survives. In the residential suite Edward III also installed England's first known supply of hot and cold water.

Richard II (1377–99) had Westminster Hall grandly remodelled by his Master Mason, Henry Yevele, and Master Carpenter, Hugh Herland, to reflect both his refined taste and his exalted view of kingship, which ultimately led to his overthrow. The walls were raised in height and refaced, and the round-headed Norman windows replaced with Gothic ones with pointed arches. A new decorative scheme featured statues of great kings and Richard II's favourite heraldic motif, the white hart. The north façade was given a striking makeover by the addition of twin towers, a vaulted porch, a huge window, and a screen of niches for statues, features more usually associated with a cathedral. The greatest triumph – of both artifice and engineering – was the

The chapel of St Mary Undercroft was originally completed in 1297 and restored by E. M. Barry in 1860–70.

installation of a mighty new hammerbeam roof, unsupported by columns, the weight being borne by stone corbels projecting from the massive walls. Prefabricated at Farnham in Surrey, 30 miles away, the woodwork was brought to Westminster by ox-cart and river. Little changed internally since then, Westminster Hall is the only part of the main medieval palace complex now surviving above ground.

The Westminster Palace apartments were devastated by fire in 1512 and abandoned by Henry VIII (1509–47) in favour of nearby Whitehall, which was in turn destroyed by fire in 1698. The law courts, however, remained in Westminster Hall, although the outside of the building was obscured by houses, taverns and coffee-houses. The Commons continued to meet in St Stephen's Chapel, which was transformed by Christopher Wren in 1692 through the addition of galleries and new windows. The number of MPs grew when representatives from Scotland (after 1707) and Ireland (after 1801) joined the Commons, and the chamber became increasingly overcrowded, overheated, uncomfortable and inconvenient.

In 1834 it was decided to dispose of the stockpile of notched wooden tallies used since the twelfth century by the Exchequer as part of its accounting system. The young Charles Dickens noted scathingly that, rather than give them away to the poor for firewood, officials ordered them burned as boiler fuel, leading to a massive fire on the night of 16–17 October 1834. Through the frantic efforts of firemen, policemen, soldiers, and boys from Westminster School, Westminster Hall was preserved. The prime minister, Lord Melbourne, commandeered cabs to carry books and precious documents saved from the flames to safety.

In June 1835 a competition was announced for designs for new Houses of Parliament, to be built on the same site, in either a Gothic or an Elizabethan style. Lying next to the venerable Gothic profile of Westminster Abbey, the new home of the legislature of the world's most rapidly modernising country was not to be a statement of architectural modernity like the functional factories, warehouses or railway stations transforming the townscapes of mid-Victorian Britain, and the classical Greco-Roman styles, then fashionable in Germany and France, were likewise rejected.

The Jewel Tower, built in 1365–6 of Kentish ragstone by Henry Yevele, is another surviving fragment of the old Palace of Westminster. Used to store the king's valuables until the reign of Henry VII, it housed parliamentary records from 1621 to 1864, and now houses an exhibition, 'Parliament Past and Present'.

A contemporary painting depicts a mass of spectators watching Parliament burn down in 1834. The painter J. M. W. Turner (1775–1851) was an eyewitness, as were his rival John Constable, the young Parliamentary reporter Charles Dickens, and both future architects of the New Palace of Westminster, Barry and Pugin.

What was wanted was an expression of the long continuity of Parliament as an institution at the heart of the nation, not a factory for churning out laws; not a 'temple of reason', but the representation in stone of history itself. Inevitably, the choice of such highly decorative styles would make its design more expensive to realise than any stripped-down functionalist or classicist alternative but, in the initial burst of enthusiasm and visionary optimism that surrounded the project, such a consideration seemed penny-pinching.

Of the ninety-seven anonymous entries submitted, ninety-one were Gothic. The competition was thus a milestone in the history of British taste, confirming Gothic as the national style for the next half century, even for secular buildings. The commission was awarded to Charles Barry (1795–1860), whose submission was exquisitely illustrated with pen and ink drawings by Augustus Pugin (1812–52). Barry had professionally trained assistants, whereas Pugin had no permanent office or support staff and was, in his own words, 'such a locomotive, being always flying about'.

In 1838 Barry accompanied an advisory group of scientists and architects on a trek in search of a suitable building stone. They settled on the Duke of Leeds's quarry at Anston in Yorkshire. This stone was good for carving but later proved to be full of flaws and has required much replacement with stone from Clipsham in Rutland and Austrude in France.

Far left: This depiction of Sir Charles Barry in the National Portrait Gallery appropriately shows him in his drawing office. Halfway through the rebuilding of the Palace of Westminster, Barry reckoned he had produced or approved nine thousand drawings.

Left: Augustus Pugin's portrait in the National Portrait Gallery includes his coat of arms and motto, *En avant* ('Forward'). The son of a French émigré artist, Pugin believed himself to be of aristocratic descent.

The foundation stone of the north front was laid in 1840 by Mrs Charles Barry. The original plan was for the work to be finished in six years at a cost of £724,896. At Barry's death in 1860 the cost had passed £2 million and the interior was still unfinished. Covering 8 acres , the buildings incorporated 1,100 rooms and 3 miles of passageways. They also required an innovatory concrete raft to stabilise the riverside foundations, and incorporated state-of-the-art fireproof iron roofing, and an advanced but immensely troublesome system of heating and ventilation, which required Barry to add the tower above the central lobby, not originally part of his approved design.

Barry's chosen style was 'Perpendicular' Gothic, a late and peculiarly English development, recalling the greatness of the Tudor age, and reflecting the specific character of Henry VII's Chapel in Westminster Abbey.

Barry's task was further complicated by the appointment of a Commission, chaired by Queen Victoria's husband, Prince Albert, 'to take into consideration the promotion of the Fine Arts of this country in connection with the rebuilding of the New Houses of Parliament'. Barry himself was excluded from membership of the Commission, which drew up an ambitious scheme for paintings and statues. Competitions to select contributing artists were held in 1843, 1844 and 1847, the winners including Daniel Maclise, C. W. Cope, Edward Armitage, William Dyce and J. C. Horsley. St Stephen's Hall now features statues of statesmen, completed between 1845 and 1858, including the first prime minister, Sir Robert

The lofty tower above the central lobby. Not part of Barry's original design, the central tower was added to aid air circulation and was imposed on him as part of the complex heating and ventilation system.

Walpole, and the youngest, William Pitt the Younger, who became prime minister aged twenty-four in 1783. Following Albert's sudden death in 1861, however, the impetus behind the fine-arts project was lost, and the Commission was wound up in 1863, having completed only a small fraction of its agenda.

Having helped Barry secure his great commission, Pugin went his own way for seven years, decorating country houses and designing churches, and even cathedrals at Birmingham, Nottingham and Southwark. In 1844 he was suddenly recalled by Barry to provide the entire decorative scheme for Parliament's interiors.

Nominally Superintendent of Wood Carving, at a niggardly £200 a year (Barry's fees ran to tens of thousands), Pugin also designed wall coverings, stained glass, tiles, textiles, metalwork, fireplaces and fittings, as well as devising Gothic forms for objects that had no medieval precedents, such as umbrella stands and gas lamps. Pugin's incredible output would have been impossible without a network of admiring, gifted and devoted collaborators who had learned to translate his inspired but often hasty sketches into fully worked-up designs – John Hardman of Birmingham for metalwork, Herbert Minton of Stoke-on-Trent for tiles, Gillow of

The crowned portcullis, symbolising security, has been the official badge of the Houses of Parliament since 1996. It was adopted as a royal emblem by Henry VII, son of Lady Margaret Beaufort, whose family badge it was. It is now used on official publications, notepaper, china and cutlery.

Statuary on the façade above the Sovereign's Entrance. Various kings and queens of England flank the central figure of Queen Victoria.

Lancaster for furniture, and J. G. Crace for paintings. Pugin's son-in-law, J. H. Powell, contributed designs for stained glass. Barry admitted Pugin's superiority as a designer; Pugin acknowledged Barry's skills as a planner and manager.

Barry, however, got the lion's share of the credit, membership of the Royal Academy and burial in Westminster Abbey. Pugin worked himself to death, dying insane at forty. The building was finally completed ten years after Barry's death under the direction of his son, Edward.

Although Gothic in style, the structure of the new Parliament building was governed by the principles of classical architecture – the Chamber of the House of Lords, for example, being a double cube 90 feet long by 45 feet high and wide. Pugin mischievously assured one enquirer that the result was 'All Grecian, Sir; Tudor details on a classic body'. The layout also reflected fundamental constitutional realities. An axial corridor with three major lobbies joins the two, clearly separated, Houses of Lords and Commons, symbolising both their collaboration and their independence from one another. The exclusion of the sovereign from the Commons – harking back to Charles I's failed attempt to arrest his parliamentary opponents – is symbolised by the installation of the throne in the House of Lords, and the creation of a separate royal access route via the Sovereign's Entrance, Sovereign's Staircase, Robing Room, Royal Gallery and Prince's Chamber.

The Robing Room, the starting point of today's official tour, is where the Queen puts on the Imperial State Crown for the State Opening of Parliament. Here E. M. Barry's fireplace features Hardman's brass figures of St George and St Michael. Dyce's frescoes illustrate Hospitality,

A cutaway depiction of the multi-layered interior of the Palace of Westminster.

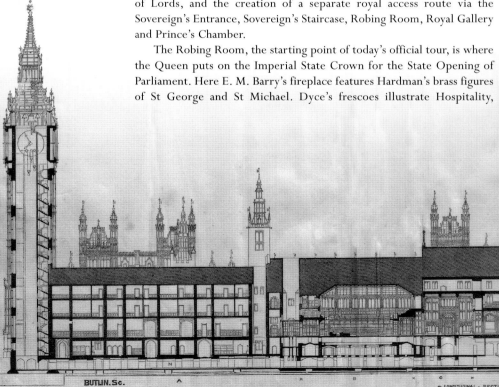

BUTLIN. Sc.

LONGITUDINAL SECTION OF THE NEW WESTMINSTER PA

Generosity, Religion, Mercy and Courtesy. Oak panels tell the story of King Arthur and Sir Galahad. Visitors then pass — as the Queen does — through the Royal Gallery, flanked by Daniel Maclise's enormous, detailed paintings of *The Meeting of Wellington and Blucher after Waterloo* and *The Death of Nelson*. The Prince's Chamber (see page 26), adjacent to the Lords, features clocks and furniture by Pugin, portraits based on

The Robing Room.

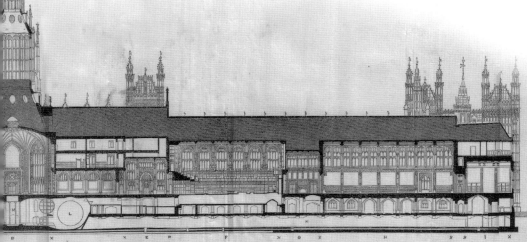

HALL - AND - BOTH - HOUSES.

FROM THE WORKING DRAWINGS.—Sir Charles Barry, R.A., Architect.

originals of Tudor royalty, and John Gibson's statue of a youthful Queen Victoria flanked by Justice and Clemency.

One of the new Parliament's earliest tourist visitors, the Anglophile American writer Nathaniel Hawthorne, was deeply impressed with Pugin's masterpiece, the House of Lords, dominated by his majestic royal throne – 'Nothing could be more magnificent and gravely gorgeous.' The upholstery is royal red. Crace's painted ceiling repeats the royal motto *Dieu et mon droit* ('[By] God and my right'). Statues between the windows represent the barons who forced King John to endorse Magna Carta and paired frescoes provide historic illustrations of virtues.

Right: The Chair of State in the Robing Room. A carved oak canopy features the rose, shamrock and thistle and the initials VR (*Victoria Regina*), which also feature in the tapestry of the Royal Arms behind the Chair of State.

Opposite, top: The Royal Gallery.

The Commons moved into its new home in 1852, the year in which Queen Victoria used the Sovereign's Entrance for the first time and knighted Charles Barry. The Commons' upholstery is green, a colour much favoured by the Plantagenets and Tudors, symbolising to the medieval mind fertility, Nature and the Christian triumph of life over death. The galleries above and behind the Speaker's Chair for the Hansard reporters and newspaper journalists constituted an architectural acknowledgement and acceptance of the legitimate presence of the 'Fourth Estate' of the realm – a free press.

In 1860 the Victoria Tower was completed, then the highest square tower in the world. Slightly taller than the more famous Clock Tower, it was constructed around an iron frame, fulfilling the design brief given to Barry to create 'a fireproof depository for books and documents', with twelve floors given over to storage. Much of the Commons' archive had perished in the fire of 1834, the Lords' documentation surviving because it was then stored in the Jewel Tower.

Following the demise of Prince Albert's commission, it was almost half a century before sustained interest in commissioning new sculptures and

Overleaf:
At 323 feet, the Victoria Tower was the tallest tower on a secular building when it was built; it now houses Parliament's archive of some three million documents, stored on 5½ miles of shelving over twelve floors, including 64,000 Acts of Parliament. It also contains a nestbox for peregrine falcons, which discourage pigeons and gulls.

paintings revived with a mural scheme for the east corridor in 1908–10, depicting the story of the Reformation. Another set, in St Stephen's Hall, executed between 1912 and 1927, illustrating *The Building of Britain*, includes, on the north wall, Charles Sims's depiction of King John assenting to Magna Carta. Mosaics (1924–6) at either end of the hall recall its history as the original home of the House of Commons from 1550 until the fire of 1834. A First World War memorial by the Australian sculptor Sir Bertram Mackennal was added to St Stephen's Porch.

The House of Commons.

Left: The Victorian House of Commons. The absence of the Mace in front of the Despatch Boxes denotes that the House is not in session. A few MPs – wearing top hats – gather beside the Speaker's chair. The chamber was rebuilt after being bombed in 1940 (see title page image).

Below: St Stephen's Hall stands where the Commons met, 1550–1834.

We here present to our readers the plan of the principal floor of the New Houses of Parliament, as now definitively decided

1. Earl Marshal
2. Sealer
3. Dressing room
4. Lord Chancellor's office
5. Messengers' room
6. Lord Chancellor
7. Dressing room
8. Clerk of Parliament
9. Peers' robing room
10. Dressing room
11. Chairman of committee
12. Secretary's room
13. Counsel room
14. Unopposed committee room
15. Select committee room
16. Doorkeeper
17. Royal staircase
18. Parliament office stairs
19. Court
20. Cabinet room
21. Housekeeper
22. Deputy Speaker
23. Members' stairs
24. Court
25. Proxy room
26. Dress room
27. Yeoman Usher
28. Staircase
29. Vote office
30. Peer's private corridor
31. Private room
32. Waiting room
33. Clerk of Parliament

34. Clerk assistant
35. Witness room
36. Witness room.
37. Witness room
38. Master in Chancery
39. Witness Room
40. Counsel
41. Ventilating office
42. Messenger
43. Waiting room
44. Clerk's office
45. Lord Great Chamberlain's room
46. Lord Great Chamberlain's dressing room
47. Writing room
48. Archbishops' room
49. Ante-room
50. Bishops' room
51. Reading room
52. Doorkeeper's dressing room
53. Peers' terrace stairs
54. Refreshment room
55. Office
56. Office
57. Office
58. Sergeant at Arms
59. Witnesses' waiting room
60. Witnesses' waiting room
61. Doorkeeper's room
62. Public petitions
63. Public petitions
64. Messenger
65. Copying office

66. Public stairs to committee rooms
67. Stationery room
68. Messenger
69. Black Rod's dining room
70. Black Rod's stairs
71. Librarian's dining room
72. Court
73. Librarian's stairs
74. Librarian's ante-room
75. Black Rod's drawing room
76. Black Rod's library
77. Librarian's drawing room
78. Refreshment
79. Public courts
80. Clerk of Committees
81. Passage
82. Clerks' office
83. Examiner and Speaker's court
84. Clerk's office
85. Examining office
86. Clerk of private bills
87. Examining office
88. Court
89. Public office for Deputy Inspector of Plans
90. Engrossment office
91. Commons private entrance
92. Messenger
93. Cloak room
94. Clerk's office
95. Vote office
96. Court
97. Refreshment

n. The original bears the signature of the architect; and we are assured that no deviation will be made from this arrangement.

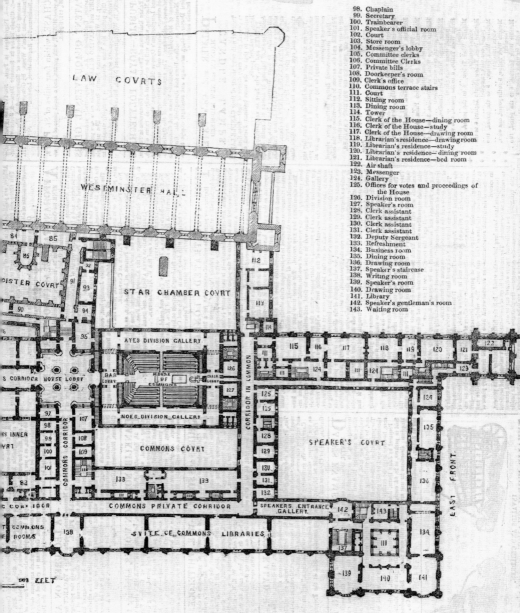

98. Chaplain
99. Secretary
100. Trainbearer
101. Speaker's official room
102. Court
103. Store room
104. Messenger's lobby
105. Committee clerks
106. Committee Clerks
107. Private bills
108. Doorkeeper's room
109. Clerk's office
110. Commons terrace stairs
111. Court
112. Sitting room
113. Dining room
114. Tower
115. Clerk of the House—dining room
116. Clerk of the House—study
117. Clerk of the House—drawing room
118. Librarian's residence—drawing room
119. Librarian's residence—study
120. Librarian's residence—dining room
121. Librarian's residence—bed room
122. Air shaft
123. Messenger
124. Gallery
125. Offices for votes and proceedings of the House
126. Division room
127. Speaker's room
128. Clerk assistant
129. Clerk assistant
130. Clerk assistant
131. Clerk assistant
132. Deputy Sergeant
133. Refreshment
134. Business room
135. Dining room
136. Drawing room
137. Speaker's staircase
138. Writing room
139. Speaker's room
140. Drawing room
141. Library
142. Speaker's gentleman's room
143. Waiting room

LAW COVRTS

WESTMINSTER HALL

CLOISTER COVRT

STAR CHAMBER COVRT

AYES DIVISION GALLERY

HOUSE OF COMMONS

BAR LOBBY

CHAIR LOBBY

HOUSE LOBBY

NOES DIVISION GALLERY

COMMONS HOVSE LOBBY

COMMONS COVRT

CORRIDOR IN COMMON

SPEAKER'S COVRT

EAST FRONT

COMMONS CORRIDOR

COMMONS INNER COVRT

COMMONS PRIVATE CORRIDOR

SPEAKERS ENTRANCE GALLERY

SVITE OF COMMONS LIBRARIES

COMMONS ROOMS

200 FEET

Previous pages:
An early plan
(1843) of the
New Palace of
Westminster, its
symmetry skewed
by the need to
incorporate
Westminster Hall.

Old Palace Yard,
May 1940, showing
extensive bomb
damage after the
last great raid of
the Blitz. Richard
the Lionheart's
sword was taken
as a sign that
democracy might
bend but would
not break.

In the octagonal central lobby the mosaic of St George, patron saint of England, dating from 1869, was matched by others of St David for Wales (1898), St Andrew for Scotland (1923) and St Patrick for Ireland (1924).

The Palace of Westminster was bombed fourteen times during the Second World War, most severely on the night of 10 May 1941, when the Chamber of the House of Commons was destroyed and the roof of Westminster Hall set alight by incendiary bombs. The Commons moved into the House of Lords for the rest of the war, and the Lords went to nearby Church House, the administrative headquarters of the Church of England.

The reconstruction of the House of Commons waited on victory but planning began in 1943. Churchill was insistent that the chamber 'should be oblong and not semicircular', to preserve the adversarial nature of debate, and that:

> It should not be big enough to contain all its Members at once without overcrowding... We attach immense importance to the survival of Parliamentary democracy ... it is one of our war aims. We wish to see our Parliament a strong, easy, flexible instrument of free Debate. For this purpose a small Chamber and a sense of intimacy are indispensable.

The task of reconstructing the House of Commons was entrusted to Sir Giles Gilbert Scott (1880–1960), President of the Royal Institute of British Architects and designer of Britain's red telephone boxes. He improved the Chamber's heating, lighting and ventilation and enlarged the galleries for visitors and the press. Additional floors, ingeniously crammed below and above the Chamber, housed new and much-needed conference rooms and offices. Scott described the task as 'an intricate business', like designing the inside of a battleship. The fire-damaged arch leading in from the Members' Lobby was retained 'as a monument to the ordeal which Westminster has passed through'. A new foundation stone was laid in May 1948 and the Chamber reopened in October 1950. Scott's revamped Commons was still Gothic, but streamlined and secular, stripped of royal symbols, such as the Tudor rose, in keeping with the temper of a modern democracy.

Twice prime minister, Sir Winston Churchill (1874–1965) was also a writer, winning the Nobel Prize for Literature. His statue on Parliament Square shows him wearing a military greatcoat; a former lieutenant-colonel in the British army, Churchill was the only British prime minister to wear uniform while in office.

PARLIAMENT AT WORK

The main task of Parliament is still what it was when first summoned, not to legislate or govern, but to secure full discussion and ventilation of all matters, legislative or administrative.

L .S. Amery, *Thoughts on the Constitution*, 1947.

THE UNITED KINGDOM is not governed *by* Parliament but *through* Parliament. The day-to-day task of governing is the work of the Cabinet and the ministers responsible for running the Exchequer, the Home Office and other departments of state; but these ministers are almost all drawn from the ranks of Parliament and are answerable to Parliament for the conduct of their business.

THE HOUSE OF COMMONS

There are 650 MPs in the House of Commons. The number varies periodically as constituency boundaries are revised to take account of the growth, decline or movement of populations. An MP must be a British subject and at least twenty-one years old. Members are elected to the House of Commons primarily as representatives of a political party, only very rarely as 'independents' on account of their particular personality or a cause they uphold. As a result most MPs vote as directed by the party 'whips', responsible for organising votes and upholding party discipline, except when there is no 'party line' to follow, or when an issue is declared to be a matter of conscience (such as capital punishment or abortion). For most of the twentieth century control of a majority in the Commons, and therefore the nature of the government in power, was in the hands of the Conservative or Labour Party. In recent decades other parties have emerged, making coalition government more likely and control of the Commons less predictable.

Members of the government and its supporters occupy the benches to the right of the Speaker, while Opposition members sit to the left, echoing and symbolising the essentially adversarial style of parliamentary politics.

Opposite:
The central lobby, where MPs may meet visitors and constituents, or talk to specialised journalists known as 'lobby correspondents'.

The war-damaged entrance to the Commons from the Members' Lobby, flanked by statues of Winston Churchill and Margaret Thatcher.

Ministers sit on the benches closest to the floor and are therefore known as 'frontbenchers', as are members of the Opposition 'shadow cabinet', who sit opposite them. Rank and file MPs sitting behind them, and not holding a position in government, are 'backbenchers' or 'private members'.

The daily business of the House of Commons begins just before 2.30 p.m. with a procession through the Central and Members' Lobbies to the Chamber, in which the Speaker is accompanied by a mace-bearer, chaplain and attendants. Onlookers are called to stand still and remove headgear as a sign of respect.

THE PARLIAMENTARY PRAYER

'The House of Commons starts its proceedings with a prayer. The chaplain looks at the assembled members ... and then prays for the country.' (Lord Denning, 1989)

The Parliamentary Prayer dates from around the beginning of the reign of Queen Elizabeth I in 1558 and was firmly established by 1567. It is said before the public are admitted and currently takes the following form:

Lord, the God of righteousness and truth, grant to our Queen and her government, to Members of Parliament and to all in positions of responsibility, the guidance of your Spirit. May they never lead the nation wrongly through love of power, desire to please or unworthy ideals, but laying aside all private interests and prejudices keep in their mind their responsibility to seek to improve the condition of all mankind; so may your kingdom come and your name be hallowed. Amen.

THE PARLIAMENTARY YEAR

November. State Opening of Parliament

December. Christmas break

January to July. Parliament in session, with brief recesses in February, at Easter and over the Spring Bank Holiday.

August. Summer recess.

September and October. End of session.

The Commons meets for about two hundred days a year, from late October until July, usually from early afternoon to late evening. On Fridays a shorter session is devoted to business raised by private members, rather than the government. MPs then usually travel back to the constituency where they were elected so that they can hold a 'surgery' in their office on Saturdays at which local people may consult them about issues that concern them. MPs do not have to live in their constituency but most have a home – or a second home – there, to demonstrate their commitment and accountability to the area and its people. The 'constituency surgery' was instituted by the post-war (1945–51) Labour government. Many MPs find helping constituents with problems such as housing or welfare benefits or their dealings with the complex machinery of government to be the most satisfying part of their job.

Proposals put before the Commons are decided by a 'division', when the House is asked to shout 'Aye' or 'No'. If the outcome is in doubt, MPs file out to be counted in person on either side, the Ayes going through the lobby on the right and the Noes on the left. 'Tellers', usually party whips, count the votes and report the result to the Speaker, who announces it to the House. In the Lords the corresponding terms are 'Content' and 'Not content'.

BILLS

A Bill is a proposal for legislation. Public bills are sponsored by the government and affect the community as a whole. Private bills are concerned with the powers or responsibilities of particular institutions, such as a local council or government agency. A Bill becomes an Act of Parliament by passing through the following stages:

First Reading. The bill is formally introduced by the government minister responsible for getting it passed, its title is read, and the bill approved ('carried') for passage to the next stage without discussion.

HANSARD

'Hansard is history's ear, already listening' (Sir Herbert Samuel, 1949).

The reporting of debates was originally banned as a breach of privilege but in 1803 newspaper reporters were allocated seats in the public gallery. From 1806 the radical agitator and journalist William Cobbett (1763–1835) began to publish regular transcripts, and from 1813 these were produced by the government printer, Thomas Curson Hansard (1776–1833), whose name remains the shorthand term for the official record of proceedings in both Houses.

Second Reading. The bill's purpose and main proposals are debated and difficulties noted.

Committee Stage. The bill is discussed in close detail in committee.

Report Stage. The committee presents the bill back to the House, which debates and accepts or rejects any changes it has made.

Third Reading. A general debate concludes the procedure. Small verbal changes may still be made but no amendments of substance.

The bill is then sent to the House of Lords to go through the same stages. A bill may also originate in the Lords and then pass through the Commons. Finally the bill is sent for the Royal Assent, which is still recorded in Norman French: *La Reine le veult* ('The Queen wills it'). Theoretically, this could be refused with the formula *La Reine s'avisera* ('The Queen will think about it'), but no monarch has refused assent for three centuries.

A Private Member's bill is sponsored by a backbench MP who has been successful in a ballot to win a Friday slot for its introduction. This gives the individual MP a rare opportunity to pursue a matter of particular concern to him or her. Usually the bill is discussed but goes no further, although this debate may attract media attention and publicity for the issue – and the MP. If the government decides to back the proposal, however, and to mobilise party votes in its support, a Private Member's Bill may pass into law. Government may take advantage of this procedure to promote a law that it favours but that may be too controversial to make part of its official programme.

COMMITTEES

Public attention and media coverage focus on the Chamber of the Commons, where debate always has the potential to turn into drama. But the main part of the Commons' work is done by committees, which examine proposed legislation in detail and investigate the performance of government.

A committee room in 1913. Its modern counterpart would be cluttered with microphones, laptops, and briefcases.

Committees usually meet in the mornings, but also when the House is sitting. They are often chaired by a member of the Opposition party and cover such areas as defence, agriculture, foreign affairs, employment, education, environment, health, and science and technology. The Public Accounts Committee reviews the efficiency of government spending.

QUESTION TIME

> I count my blessings ... that I don't have to go into that pit ... nose to nose with the Opposition, all yelling at each other. (President George Bush, Senior)

MPs regularly submit written questions to the government about its conduct of business. The first hour of parliamentary business from Monday to Thursday is taken up by Question Time, when government ministers (on Wednesdays the prime minister) answer questions put by MPs. The Despatch Boxes are the brassbound oak boxes on which ministers and senior Opposition spokesmen may lean and rest their notes when speaking. They contain the Bibles used for swearing in new MPs. The present boxes are the gift of New Zealand, to replace those destroyed in the Blitz.

Parliamentary questions must be 'tabled' beforehand, but after the minister has delivered his carefully prepared answer he or she must then respond to a 'supplementary' question, which can only be guessed at. Questions put by MPs from the government party are usually intended to help it show its achievements in a positive light. Opposition questions aim to trap or trick ministers into revealing their shortcomings. Good performers

Overleaf: Speaker John Bercow surveys MPs at the beginning of a new parliamentary session.

who are witty and relaxed 'at the Despatch Box' are widely admired on all sides — but that does not mean that they are necessarily better at running a government department.

MR SPEAKER

The Speaker presides over the debates of the House of Commons to ensure good order. MPs bow slightly to the Speaker's Chair on entering and leaving the Commons Chamber as a sign of respect for the House. The Speaker, who is chosen by the House, may be from the government or Opposition party and may serve for many years. The Speaker votes only to break a tie.

The Speaker's House occupies the corner of the Palace of Westminster nearest to Westminster Bridge. Apart from being a domestic residence, it is also used for official entertaining. At the other corner of the Palace, facing on to the river, are the apartments of the Lord Speaker, who presides over the debates of the House of Lords.

The Mace, originally a club used as a weapon of war, evolved into an elaborate symbol of the authority of the House of Commons. Carried in by the Serjeant-at-Arms, it is removed when the Speaker vacates his chair, to show that the House is no longer in session. The present Mace dates from the reign of Charles II. Similar maces are found in parliaments throughout the English-speaking world.

THE PARLIAMENTARY DAY

Monday and Tuesday

2.30 The Speaker arrives in the Commons Chamber in a procession from the Speaker's House. The Speaker's Chaplain leads prayers.

2.35 – 3.30 Question Time.

3.30 Statements by ministers. Points of order addressed to the Speaker.
    Beginning of main business.

10.00 – 10.30 'Adjournment debate' on a subject raised by a backbencher.

Wednesday

Timings are three hours earlier, with prime minister's questions from 12.00 to 12.30.

Thursday

Timings are four hours earlier.

Friday

The House meets at 9.30 and adjourns at 3.00 or shortly after.

PROPER BEHAVIOUR

The *Treatise on the Law, Privileges, Proceedings and Usages of Parliament*, compiled by Thomas Erskine May (1815–86), has been the definitive guide to parliamentary procedure and customs since its publication in 1844. May wrote the first nine editions himself.

May advised that 'Good temper and moderation are the characteristics of Parliamentary language'. Members may not accuse each other of hypocrisy, drunkenness or false motives, misrepresent what another has said, use abusive or insulting language, or lie deliberately, although, as Norman Tebbitt noted in 1991, 'Parliament must not be told a direct untruth but it is quite possible to allow them to mislead themselves'. Banned terms include 'coward', 'traitor', 'hooligan', 'swine', 'rat', 'guttersnipe' and 'git'. Offenders may be singled out by the Speaker and 'named'. A first offence merits five days' exclusion and loss of salary, a second twenty days, and a third a punishment decided by the House.

Members are referred to by their constituency, not by name – 'the Honourable Member for …', unless they are ministers, in which case they are identified by their office as 'the Secretary of State for …' privy councillors and senior ministers are additionally referred to as 'the Right Honourable'. Members speak only if called to do so by the Speaker, and stand up while speaking. They are not normally allowed to speak twice on the same topic. Notes are allowed, but members should talk rather than read out a prepared speech.

MPs respectfully await the announcement of the election of the Speaker who will moderate their debates.

Portcullis House,
designed by
Michael Hopkins
and completed
in 2000, enabled
every MP to have
an individual office
for the first time.
It also houses
additional
committee rooms
and refreshment
facilities.

Members may not bring briefcases into the House, read letters or newspapers, or drink, eat or smoke – although a box of snuff is set by the entrance to the chamber for their use. A jacket and tie are required for male members, though most wear dark lounge suits. In the Members' Cloakroom there are still swags of pink ribbon for members to hang up their swords. The wearing of hats or military medals is forbidden.

SPACE AND STAFF

Compared to lawmakers in other countries, Westminster MPs have not been well resourced in terms of office space and support staff. Charles Barry's brief did not cover these, leading to a century of overcrowding and improvisation. The first steel filing cabinet arrived in 1931, the first female typist in 1932. Only since the completion of Portcullis House in 2000 has every MP had his or her own individual office. Most peers still have no office.

THE HOUSE OF LORDS

Britain was unique in the twentieth century in retaining within its democratically elected Parliament an entire chamber in which the majority of its members sat by right of birth, not by election, or even by appointment. Most of the hereditary members, however, stayed away most of the time, leading Sir Herbert Samuel to observe in 1948 that 'The House of Lords must be the only institution in the world which is kept efficient by the persistent absenteeism of most of its members.' The preamble to the 1911 Parliament Act, limiting the powers of the House of Lords, made it clear that it was a temporary compromise pending the substitution of 'a second chamber constituted on a popular instead of a hereditary basis'. A century later, this has still not been achieved. Instead new members have been added by the creation of 'Life Peers', appointed by the prime minister in consultation with other party leaders; in 1999 the number of 'hereditaries' was reduced to a rump of ninety-two. The fact that Life Peers are appointed has at least made it possible to make the membership a better reflection of British society by increasing the number of female and ethnic minority members.

The present House of Lords consists of some 750 members, of whom about 630 are life peers. Other members include the Archbishops of Canterbury and York and the twenty-four most senior bishops of the Church of England, and ninety-two hereditary peers, elected by their fellows from a pool of some seven hundred titled members of the nobility. The ninety-two include the Lord Great Chamberlain, who serves as the Queen's representative in the Lords, and the Earl Marshal, responsible for ceremonies, notably the State Opening of Parliament.

The Lord Speaker sits on a large, red bale of wool. In the Middle Ages England was a major exporter of wool, which therefore symbolised the wealth of the nation. Remade after wartime damage, the Woolsack was

The throne in the House of Lords, with the Woolsack in the foreground. (see also the cover image).

stuffed with wool from Australia, New Zealand and other Commonwealth countries as a symbol of Commonwealth unity and the attachment of its members to Westminster traditions.

Like the Commons, the House of Lords holds debates and considers the details of legislation. Party discipline is less tight than in the Commons, and many peers are 'crossbenchers', independent of a party whip.

BLACK ROD

The office of Gentleman Usher of the Black Rod was established by royal patent in 1350 and acquired its present title in 1522, reflecting the holder's symbol of authority, an ebony staff topped with a golden lion. Technically the personal attendant of the sovereign when in the House of Lords, Black Rod has day-to-day responsibility for its security, and dealing with any disorder or disturbance. The appointment is held by a former general, admiral or air marshal. The Serjeant-at-Arms is his counterpart in the

Black Rod summons MPs to the House of Lords to hear the Queen's Speech at the State Opening of Parliament.

The Sovereign's Entrance to the Victoria Tower is used by the Queen at the State Opening of Parliament.

THE OPENING OF PARLIAMENT.

The State Opening of Parliament. The State Coach is escorted by Yeomen of the Guard and cavalry of the Household Division.

House of Commons. The upper houses of the parliaments of Canada, Australia and New Zealand all have their own Black Rod.

Queen Elizabeth II reading the Queen's Speech during a State Opening of Parliament.

THE STATE OPENING OF PARLIAMENT

The State Opening is the elaborate ceremony in which the monarch comes in person, usually in late autumn, to inaugurate the annual parliamentary session. Wearing the Imperial State Crown, the Queen occupies the throne in the House of Lords. MPs are summoned from the House of Commons to hear her read the 'Queen's Speech', which is drafted by the government, setting out its proposed programme of legislation.

Black Rod is sent to the House of Commons to summon MPs to hear the Queen's Speech read in the 'House of Peers'. By tradition the door is slammed in Black Rod's face, to symbolise the independence of the House of Commons, and as a reminder of Charles I's failed attempt to arrest the five members he had singled out as leaders of the opposition to his rule. Black Rod knocks with his staff three times on the door of the Commons, which then opens for MPs to process through to the Lords.

VISITING PARLIAMENT

FOR REASONS OF SECURITY and efficiency, most rooms in the Palace of Westminster are off limits to visitors. The river frontage houses — in sequence from the Lord Speaker's apartments to the Speaker's Residence — the extensive House of Lords' Library, the much smaller Lords' Guest Room and Pugin Room, with the best-known portrait of the architect, the Strangers' (visitors') Dining Room, the Members' Dining Room, and the House of Commons Library.

The Parliament Square frontage houses the Clerks of the Parliament, above the Chancellor's Gate entrance, and Ministers' Rooms, beyond the Peers Entrance and in the shadow of the clock tower. Two sequences of courtyards provide light and ventilation. Behind the river frontage, running from the Lord Speaker's apartments, they are Royal Court, Peers' Court, Peers' Inner Court, Commons Inner Court, Commons Court and Speaker's Court. On the other side of the palace the sequence runs from Chancellor's

Court, through State Officers' Court, St Stephen's Court and Cloister Court to reach Star Chamber Court, whose name recalls the much-feared secret tribunal used by Tudor and Stuart kings to punish offenders whose wealth or status put them beyond the reach of the regular courts.

Visitors do, however, see two locations crucial to the functioning of Parliament. In the central lobby, MPs meet constituents seeking their aid, or representatives of interest groups or pressure groups 'lobbying' for their support or influence in raising a matter for debate or affecting details of proposed legislation. In the Members' Lobby MPs meet informally with the hundred or so 'lobby correspondents' – accredited journalists specialising in reporting parliamentary proceedings and personalities. The Members' Lobby is dominated by statues and busts of past prime ministers, notably Sir Winston Churchill, David Lloyd George and Margaret Thatcher.

Tours (75 minutes, wheelchair accessible) are available on Saturdays all year round (9.15 a.m. to 4.30 p.m.) and, when Parliament is in recess, from the end of July to early September (weekdays, except Wednesday mornings), and in the second half of September (all day Monday and Friday, otherwise afternoons only). For groups of ten or more the 9.15 tour is cheaper than

The river frontage of the New Palace of Westminster runs for 872 feet. The riverside location was influenced by the Duke of Wellington's advice: 'You must build up your House of Parliament upon the river; so ... that the populace cannot exact their demands by sitting down round you.'

The otherwise grand offices of the Commonwealth Parliamentary Association are dwarfed by their gargantuan neighbour.

A Sunday morning in the 1950s at Speakers' Corner, Marble Arch. Speakers may talk on any topic providing they are at least a foot off the ground, to forestall objections more forcible than heckling. Dating from the 1860s, Speakers' Corner has been copied in several Commonwealth countries.

later tours. Tours in French, German, Spanish and Italian are available at specific times. Photography is not permitted except in Westminster Hall, where there is an information desk, with public lavatories and the Jubilee Café opposite.

For tickets and further information visit: www.ticketmaster.co.uk/housesofparliament

FURTHER READING AND WEBSITES

Baldwin, N. (editor). *Parliament in the Twenty-First Century*. Politico's, 2005.

Field, John. *The Story of Parliament in the Palace of Westminster*. Politico's and James & James, 2002.

Hill, Rosemary. *God's Architect: Pugin and the Building of Romantic Britain*. Penguin, 2008.

Jones, Bill, and Norton, Philip. *Politics UK*. Longman, seventh edition, 2010.

Mitchell, Austin. *Parliament in Pictures*. Thames & Hudson, 1999.

Norton, Philip. *Parliament in British Politics*. Palgrave, 2005.

Rogers, Robert. *Order! Order!: A Parliamentary Miscellany*. JR Books, 2009.

Rogers, Robert, and Walters, Rhodri. *How Parliament Works*. Longman, sixth edition, 2006.

Ross, Iain (editor). *The Houses of Parliament: History, Art, Architecture*. Merrell, 2000.

Rush, Michael. *Parliament Today*. Manchester University Press, 2005.

Tames, Richard. *Political London: A Capital History*. Historical Publications, 2007.

The Times Guide to the House of Commons. Times Books, annual editions.

Wilson, Robert. *The Houses of Parliament*. Pitkin, 2006.

ORGANISATIONS

Commonwealth Parliamentary Association: www.cpahq.org

Electoral Reform Society: www.electoral-reform.org.uk

Hansard Society for Parliamentary Government:
    www.hansardsociety.org.uk

The Parliamentary Bookshop: www.bookshop@parliament.uk

WEBSITES

www.parliament.uk

www.parliamentlive.tv

www.histparl.ac.uk

www.historyofparliamentonline.org

www.bbc.co.uk/history/trail/church-state/westminster-palace/change-palace-westmin-01.shtml

www.explore-parliament.net

www.parliament.uk/factsheets

www.parliament.uk/about/visiting.cfm

INDEX